Lives of the APOSTLES

Clif Collins

PAGE PUBLISHING, INC.
New York, NY

First originally published by Page Publishing, Inc. 2017

ISBN 978-1-64082-159-0 (Paperback)
ISBN 978-1-64082-160-6 (Digital)

Printed in the United States of America

for Eileen

'Either he is talking, or he is
pursuing, or he is in a journey,
or peradventure he sleepeth,
and must be awaked.'
—1 Kings 18:27

And the things you can't remember
tell the things you can't forget
that history puts a saint in every dream.
—Tom Waits

CONTENTS

18 Movements

1. Hunger
2. Spoke as a Child
3. Desert Voices
4. Laughter in the Next Room
5. Lost Prophets
6. Ashes
7. Given Sight
8. Having Looked upon the Dead
9. Deception
10. The Walls
11. Exiles
12. Whose Name Is in the Language
13. A Different Season
14. Wandering Spring
15. History Answers
16. Following a Life
17. Elegies
18. The Spoken Word

THE LOST PROPHET

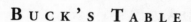

BUCK'S TABLE

Old guy wore every day
of his sixty-something years
scuffed as an old boot heel
from all that time
running long hauls, he said.

One night, we were standing
outside Betty's Lounge,
would've been thirty years ago
at least, and we
were passing a joint

back and forth, watching
the train disappear
while we waited
on a game of eight ball,

and he said how if he could
just find the right woman
he'd burn everything
he owned and start over,

then laughed and freed
the smoke on that kudzu trestle—
said that's what he'd been doing
most of his life anyway,
minus the right woman.

SUNDAY MORNING, 11:00

Heavy-hipped and slow-flowing
in those floor-length skirts
of many colors, where's Ninah—

Don't worry about that now
you a big boy, just sit up straight . . .

coffee and apple snuff on her breath?

. . . pay attention and don't laugh
when the preacher repeats himself,
he's old.

Wide laughing lap and hands
rough as any man's but easy too
and cornrows you can touch
with yellow green orange
plastic bows . . .

Draw pictures in the bulletin
if you have to then,
but stand up for the hymns
and least learn to lip
the words to the Nicene Creed.

PATRILINEAL QUESTION, 1968

Cancer in his bladder and dust
on the fields, he died three days
shy of my sixth birthday,
died on the dull edge of morphine
in the front bedroom

just off the screen porch
where old men now sat
smoking cigarettes and sweating
through their shirt sleeves,
leaning forward with elbows
on their knees as they revisited
the Great Depression until finally

somebody thought to bring out
an electric fan, one made
with salvaged parts from the planes
he'd serviced out at the airfield,
and the men nodded and said how
he could make damn near anything
because making was in his hands.

Died late in the afternoon
on the last Sunday in August
with the sun just starting to settle
over 112 acres of soy beans.

Three days later I stood alone
watching the car pull away
down that long dirt road
toward the highway, that same dust
blown into the pecan trees
and the wife of a family friend
promising iced tea and sugar cookies
if I'd just come back in the house.

But the questions were all outside
that morning, waiting patiently
with their black wings folded
high up in the branches—

where would all his stories go now,
the secret songs and jokes
our mothers wouldn't let us hear,
and what would they do
with his name, which was also
my name, now he was dead?

VARDAMAN DREAMS OF ELECTION DAY

Who is fire bill three-oh-six-one-four,
Darl, and why do people want to kill him?
Does he live in fire, Darl, is that who he is,
and do you have a number too?
There are five of them flapping
their wings now, saying family family
Flag. . .flag family flag
sometimes flag wins and sometimes
family and they all smile God
and the congress man is aunty inflation,
only he's no lady, not the fat lady
either but says he's against new texas,
which is like new mexico, but says no
to texas, so very soon now
the fat lady will sing Davy Crockett
and if you was to vote, Darl, you
could vote for me, I'll bet, so then I
could be elect too, and who are
the elect, Darl? who are the elect?

WILLIE MCTELL (1898–1959)

I could smell the rain
coming across the fields
and know sound was next,
how one thing follows another,
same way you can hear
a straight-8

two miles down the road
just before the tires
are right there about ready
to haul you off
with that steady hum

running time through
your bones, saying
Let it be heard,
so I left everything behind
then, all but the 12-string,
one for each apostle,

and walked out into a world
just now waking up—
those big doors creaking shut
on the cotton houses, dogs
barking and horns blowing
through the wind off Decatur—

all that space in between
I knew wasn't empty
cause I could hear even before
I touched it, the word living
alongside every sound.

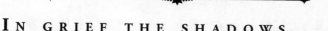

IN GRIEF THE SHADOWS . . .

In grief the shadows
of your face came alive,
the bones terrifying
and beautiful.
I had never
seen you this way
and tried not to look.
Forgive the intrusion,
the old man in the hat
standing at your door.
It was sorrow
that brought him there
empty-handed
and without words.

St. Paul Street, 1985

Walking all hours North Avenue
up to 33rd, Bo Peep knows
every marble stoop
and liquor store and steeple—
hangs in the shadows
of small-time dealers
and crack whores
'Too broke to pay attention'
he says, so they laugh
and tell him go check his pulse
by the blinking Bud sign
in the window over on Charles.
Some nights he stands outside
the laundromat watching
the dryers spin
one month to the next
and he'll hitch up his pants
with the cuffs piled
over the shoe tops and
scratch at that beard
he borrowed off Methuselah
or Tolstoy, or maybe an architect.
He was living deep
in the plate glass of the blood bank
one afternoon in March
when a cop came out
and asked if he was looking for
anyone in particular
and Bo Peep told him yeah
but he hadn't seen him in years.

WINTER BIRCHES

If the sky were a desert,
you'd likely find here
a sun-bleached skull
from an animal who died
long ago believing in water,
a hinged mandible
you could open and shut
and give your own words:
Yes, February, Mrs. Merson—
it is easy see them now
lined up across the highway
for their long procession into
the land of the undreaming.

MUNCHAUSEN BY PROXY

Is this then what the martyrs felt
in the last moments of their undoing,
the stares of disbelief
with their spirits broken
and their pain seizing in the dust—
this and nothing more their portion?
And no revelation in it, of course,
a few parched words maybe,
nothing else even to pretend.
Curled up in a chair, all she'll say is
how she thought maybe it was colic
this time and she spent
two whole days on that stencil
just above the crib,
Mommy's Little Angel:
a teddy bear with big curious eyes
and a halo, like he wonders why . . .

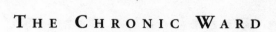

THE CHRONIC WARD

The appaloosa you trained
when you were ten,
a patient metaphor:
children and lunatics nearer God.
Nearer My God to Thee
Thursdays at noon,
playing Rorschach with a bird
in the minute hand,
and his mad monk eyes
worth two, see-saw bounce
and chase your stockings
all the way from tippy-toe
to never-never land

MY BROTHER'S NIETZSCHE

All that winter we rode our bikes
through the mottled half-light
of first-growth timber, holding fast
to a trail cut through by the power company,
bracing our tires over the deep frozen tracks
of dozers and skirting the jagged seams left open
from tree roots torn out by logging chains—

half a mile deep off the highway
to the black-iron-brick fence where inside
they let her walk the halls sometimes
in a lime-green housecoat, he said, the woman
who'd fed three-quarters of her family Terro,
pushing 260 now, having dodged the chair
over in Jackson all those years.

The wheelchairs were rolled out at four
each day, their faces squinting in the sun
like newborn babies, he said, heads lolling
while their mouths moved soundless
as summer cattle on the cud and somewhere
back in those walls she kept company
with Lee Harvey Oswald and Mata Hari, maybe
even the Seven goddamn Dwarves, he said.

Not even so much as a glimpse, though,
for all the hours we sat with that February wind
carving up the tree line and whittling away
our want for just anything
so we could tell them all, whoever said
she wasn't hardly human,
that she sure wasn't make-believe
either, and maybe then
they'd have to answer for her being.

THE BREAKER BOY (1908)

Who will rise with me
before the sun
and warm my boots
and mend my coat
for another day,
and wrap my bread
and walk the County Road
to the Erie Mine
to pick the dirt and slate
from the shuffling coal?
Another year or so,
my work stays true,
I'll have a man's wage
when I turn fourteen,
a dollar a day
driving the Erie mules.

VIEW FROM AN APARTMENT WINDOW

On some warm
spring evening
when you are 22 or so,
and dusk pushes in
through an open window
where curtains swell
and billow, and books
are stacked, and bills
are paid, and even
an old typewriter
seems just possible—and
all of this and Baltimore
now is you—
it's as yet inconceivable
that one day mortality
will mean you too.

N E R U D A ' S T I M E

In that little room
on the Jersey side
of the Lincoln Tunnel
eyes tightened
on all discordant things—
cracked mirrors, spinal cords
and eighteen wheelers—
blood playing
to the rush of traffic
while the air-conditioner
swallowed cars
all those years ago:
May come what, time will,
arched in gasps
and recollections.
And I would give you
my mouth again, and you
the taste of a myth to live by
again, and every word
a lament inside the hour
of your hips then-rising.

THE HARVESTERS AT YPRES

(from a letter to James Hodge, Hickory, NC, 1924)

. . . As I sat this morning drinking coffee
and watching Emil's family
gather vegetables,
I remembered you telling of the nuns
at Calais with their backs
bent over dying soldiers
and nothing to be done, really, but to expect
a miracle. I see only one so far.
You must return soon, mon frère,
and see Lazarus brought to the land.
Such bounty you cannot believe.
Emil will be happy to lend you a shovel.
He has an extra after his nephew
dug up another jaw
in the onion field last week.

HEART ATTACK SKY

We got our circles whooping overhead,
clearing out the cowboy clouds
and rounding up stars before anyone
has time to miss them,
and I don't care anymore
if the sky collapses or the Tin Man dies,
I just want to ride thumbs-up forever
on oxygen and *be there soon.*

LINES SPOKEN FOR CLYDE BARROW IN DOAK SIDWELL'S BAR

(Garland, Texas 1934)

There was trouble plenty
in that crooked-boy smile
and more than enough meanness
once his eyes had narrowed
down that long barrel,
trying to find Christ
in the crosshairs maybe—

he was too far gone for reason by then.

Too many days turned to a blind wall
where nothing breathes nor even
belongs to its own skin anymore,

just a rage fast rising
to cut its own destruction,
like the Brazos down around Brogan
come September,

or the road through Bienville Parish

grown still but for the buzzing of flies
and the far-off hum of a V-8,
death waiting there
in the high grass, patient as Job.

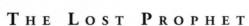

THE LOST PROPHET

And I will stand before you with words
You will not understand and so will first rebuke.
For you have been taught in ways unbefitting a believer,
Indeed have not been taught at all
But only told such as meets your pride
And will therefore one day be your own destruction.
I say to you now, Do not look outside for your enemy;
He is not there, nor does he dwell alone in your streets.
Rather, understand first what is in your heart
So that you may renounce its iniquities
And the blindness to which they have led you,
Knowing therefore the wisdom of that which I ask:
To stay the hand that would strike in retribution,
And hold the tongue whose words are sown in lies.
For surely guilt is with you as it rests upon all men.
Therefore should you live always, in word and deed,
With humility as an expression of your unknowing.

THE HORN
PLAYER'S VERSE

UNREQUITED (IN THE PARK THAT DAY)

In the Park that day
there were bright bassoons;
sun ducks swam
their summer circles
and Sunday girls
in Zelda dresses ordered tea.

A silver unicycle
hesitated,
balanced on the sun, while
clop-horse carriages rocked by.

In a quiet spot, memory sat
reading an old newspaper,
equal parts longing and regret,
where some long afternoons
I came for you.

There was a wooden bench too,
just east of the fountain,
and while he tuned
a two-dollar toy guitar

to Spanish C,
she sat sideways
with her feet in his lap
and read aloud Neruda.

COUNTY DUMP

At thirteen, I counted myself a skeptic
bound for a life of committed atheism
and an eternity, the Methodist preacher
assured me, in the deepest recesses of hell,
when my friend Oscar found
a ruined pipe wrench
one Saturday at the county dump.
He lived across the road in the last
of the half-dozen sharecropper shacks
left over from Reconstruction days,
tumble-down-looking places
that bore the full weight
of unstirring fetid air beside the highway.
While I stood in the truck bed
that morning, tossing out
moldy boat cushions, grease rags,
bait containers, and old tractor parts—
pretty much anything, really, the years
could pile up in a storage barn—
my old man paid three dollars
for a rusted-out wrench with the jaw
frozen solid and I wondered
if soft-headedness was in my blood
along with green eyes and a receding hairline.

Seething in a way that only comes
through ninety-degree heat
radiating out of garbage stink, I told him
he'd never be able to fix
that fucked-up excuse of a wrench,
would never see a moment's use from the thing,
and he said what he always said
whenever he didn't feel like explaining,
'Expect not,' and stowed it under
the driver's seat for the next fifteen years.

RUDY JOKING (1964)

Rudy laughs
cause if he don't
they'll know it's true

and knowing's different
than just thinking

that somebody
that everybody
keeps talking about

is you

and Rudy's daddy
knows someone
who knows a doctor
whose specialty is

the knife's precision
and the needle's poke,

a magician, really,
with electrodes, *poof!*

so a mind vanishes
in tiny clouds
of hospital smoke

A WOMAN WHO PLAYED THE BASS FIDDLE

A woman who played the bass fiddle
Strung years into musical riddles,
    The strangest of words
    Fed to exotic birds
And they'd sing the whole coot and kabiddle.

COME HOME SONG: 134TH AND PARK, 1920

Coleman said how that hophead cornet
who'd sweat through to the razor
he kept hidden on a string,
him and those drummer twins—
with them it was always play, pray,
and keep your head down low,
so most nights his eyes stayed
fixed to his own bell, matching
each glint off the brass
to a single note, *spark valve c*,
kiss his black ass and percussion
be damned.
How crazy it was over there,
he said, people wouldn't believe
that sound and took to studying
his trumpet so close you'd a thought
they was trying to play it with an eye socket
and only two Creoles half understanding
what they was saying in the first place.
Looking up some nights, he couldn't see
past the lights, just a sketch of body
with maybe a hand flashing out,
but knew anyway
all those eyes staring full-on
so he remembered the church on Lenox
when he was a kid, organs forever
burning saints into the wall,
and Coleman said how even now
it was like his horn kept reminding him
can't nobody live in that fire too awful long.

SEPARATING

All the way down King's Mountain
we coasted, cheating the gas man,
teasing the brakes just enough
to hold the road while you stared
out of your separate quiet
at the trees sliding past,
and the baby laughed in the backseat,
waving at birds, as yet tucked away
from the self-deception, betrayal, lies
eating away at three lives now,
the wind in my ear whispering
secret epiphanies about reaping fruit
and the bed you lie in until I heard
the strange broken truth of my own voice:
I cannot believe in you anymore.

HARD PLASTIC EYES

The afternoon I first arrived, a newly stamped
petty criminal in Mrs. Nolan Lee's living room,
she wore a checkered blue pinafore with a white bow.
Mrs. Nolan Lee said I would be a gentleman host
then disappeared upstairs for most of the week
with instructions to look presentable
and welcome visitors, if any showed:
the wages of sin, I guess,
for jimmying open a school gym window,
me and a dozen likeminded shirts and skins,
one rainy Sunday afternoon
when the principal showed up with the police.
While other offenders scrubbed walls
or picked up trash along the roads—
giant green baggies filled with garbage speared
by an eight-penny nail on a broom handle—
I sat the second week of December
in a room full of dolls no one came to see.
Hundreds of them, sitting splay-legged
on rocking chairs, divans, and sofas,
standing with a metal brace up their spine
on windowsills or tucked into bookshelves.
The rarest and most favored were coffined
in large glass cases floor to ceiling,
porcelain dolls from Mrs. Nolan Lee's childhood,
dolls with real human hair and lace-up boots
and eyelids that moved in their antique collars.

Dresses: velvet, gingham, muslin, silk.
Some had their names on folded white cards,
others a small tag that gave their birthplace
in Stockholm, St. Louis, San Francisco, Berlin.
But it was the eyes—frozen and dead
and still watching anyway—that put a mark
of guilt on you no matter where you sat, so many
unblinking stares there was no place of refuge
in that house, no place to go without being seen.

TROPICAL STILLBIRTH

I have stood in the hollow place
where infants are left to the wind,
where smoke curls up the color
of marrow into a bloodless sky.
Nothing is familiar there
but for the dry ground
where dreams burrow
and the moon is all night long
dripping children into the sea.
The wind here is to all things alike,
a void where even memory goes
once it has taken its first swallow,
lying wide-eyed in an empty room
at two a.m., waiting to be named.

IF YOU WANT TO UNDERSTAND . . .

If you want to understand the weight of lies,
just remember the light touch of snow
on your face that winter and stories told
so often you actually believed them—
told in a cow-eyed sadness
with every muscle taut to the threat
of discovery—and when I tried to tell you
no, you wouldn't believe me,
so much faith you had
in desert flowers and the changes of youth.
Now when I see the thickness of years
on your body, the abandonment of yourself
to the bitterness you've become,
I know God has mercy in giving you
names to take the place of your own,
nightshade and jimson weed to keep you
from the true ravages of introspection.

TWO-STORY HOUSE, 1958

A quarter mile off the interstate
this two-story brick house
sits empty on old 49, right across
from a defunct filling station
where locals lounged for sixty years,
changing tires and bearings
and gauging the world
one day to the next.

The first story is where
the family sat while the father
played Brahms on the piano
for his two daughters,
and the mother served lemonade
and everyone called it 1958,
a taffeta dress folded away
for the perfect Christmas
that would never come.

Because it's the second story
no one tells: how the old man
took each daughter separately
out to the farm and blew her head off
before turning the .410 on himself
the Saturday after Thanksgiving.

He took something else
that day too,
from a kid nobody remembers
standing on the drugstore sidewalk,
age seventeen when he heard it
and November kicked up
the way it can around here,
a blasting wind blowing wild
with leaves and candy wrappers
and words that sounded far off
exploding in his spine.

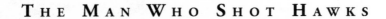

THE MAN WHO SHOT HAWKS

With the Saved Sinner front tag
and a 20-gauge in the trunk,
he drove his gold Mercury
two hours south, to a field
he'd baited for quail.
And finding the earth's hunters
had arrived as well, great birds
drawn there for survival,

he shot them down
one by one
for their interloping wings,
half a dozen or so
planted where they fell.
God gave man dominion
over all the earth, he said then,
glorious ignorance Personified,
oblivious in the way of all hypocrites.

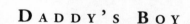

DADDY'S BOY

We'd hide our faces
behind lunch boxes and backpacks
every day Robbie Dyson
came to school in the fifth grade,
hair slicked back
with handfuls of Vitalis
that couldn't hide the smell
of cigarettes and heating oil
in the winter,
fried meat come spring,
a regular year-round stink
shifting with the seasons,
slinking alone down the hallways
in shoes so big they curled up
like a clown's.
Just random pieces
cobbled together, that was
Robbie Dyson, so we laughed
and called him Elvis—
asked if his sisters lived inside
that knee-length jacket,
sleeves swallowing his hands.
Someone whispered how
all those odd-fitting clothes
had belonged to his old man,
a part-time mechanic
and full-time drunk who'd
lit out for Mobile back in March.

Disliked even by the teachers
for his poverty and ignorance,
sometimes Robbie would get
runt-mad and want to fight
out on the playground,
but nobody wanted to fight
Robbie Dyson, not even the girls,
afraid they might actually hurt him,
this bony-ass kid trying
any way he could just to hold on.

MEMORY: THE EGG
HUNTERS (1975)

Thirty years returned from a war
he'd never left and too pickled to die, Uncle Doyle
said the first casualty of combat was the eyes,
by then gone milky and opaque,
weighed down by the stillness and half moons
in which he dreamed and drank Old Crow,
watched Walter Cronkite every night at six thirty.

Resurrection tales he had no use for,
not wafers or grape juice, nor the vague shapes
dressed like dyed eggs bouncing around his yard,
parting pyracantha and shaking dogwood limbs.
'Ought to get those eyes looked at, Doyle,'
his brothers told him, 'before they're completely gone,'
not seeing that somewhere in there
was just enough room to hide
so he kept from walking off the edge completely
else eating a twelve-gauge some night in his own garage.

Clean-up detail some high-brass sonofabitch
had called it back then, while a corporal showed him
how to tie a handkerchief around his face
so the rot plastered to his throat
could fall back and burrow in through the pores.
A sergeant from Stillwater told him the second day
there was just too much to bury,
then turned his .45 on a German guard,
a skinny blond kid still trying to puzzle out the trees.

He was still hearing the quake of dozers, could smell
diesel mixed in with the freshly turned ground
two weeks later when Barton was telling him
about the Polish woman kept alive on quarter GI rations
and canteen water, then showed Doyle a religious tract
with block letters asking Have You Been Saved?
Barton's West Texas voice was steady as a psalm
with the excitement running hard underneath
like some secret language of desert springs
imparted to the prophets to be passed down
and inherited from his Pentecostal daddy

so maybe it was true after all, Barton said,
that there really was some kind of redemption
could be found most anywhere, and surely by them
if promised to a blind Ukrainian or the Norwegian student
or the white-haired Gypsy who quoted Rimbaud.
This would be Doyle's last clear memory of religion
or Ronald Barton either one,
flaming red eyebrows over a freckled nose
and those golly-gee green eyes gone wide
as cartoon question marks when Doyle
handed him back the brochure and set out for the latrine.

GRANDDADDY JOE

Granddaddy, Granddaddy,
sick body smell
dying in the back room
with nobody to tell
the self-loathing, hatred
and bone-blind shame,
a thousand crippled memories,

a bastard for your name.
A razor strop
and steel-toed boot—was that
him or you?—and Lord knows
there'd be plenty to tell
if they would only listen
and you could only speak.

Time is like that, plodding,
intractable as an old cow
chewing away toward oblivion,
and if there are words for it
moldering in a ditch somewhere,
they were pitched there years ago
and nobody much cares anyhow.

OPHELIA'S DREAM

Who knows sees what
the broken mind beholds:
lost stars and lemon trees.

In sleep only, she sees
the garden transformed.

An old Syrian living
alone in the desert
draws ash from his fire,

scratches prayers
in the earth
with a cypress stick

so the eyes of all dead infants
may be returned to God.

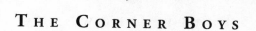

THE CORNER BOYS

North Calvert and 25th,
these corner boys
hanging quiet on Sunday
like they done found
an answer up in here
and can't none of them
be seen, all super-hero invisible
and shit with that wife-beater tee,
low-slung jeans
and Jordans, and no more
to it than just a nod
so you know they got
whatever it is you wanting
(long as you ain't
a Walmart hoodie
greasing out the Five-0,
a.k.a. John Law, Johnny Popo)
so yeah okay cool,
in the alley right behind
the Korean place,
ain't holding but can
have it here in under ten,
cause it's the first rule
of the hustle, old and beat
and always, son:
keep it neat and discreet
and your shit out the street.

R I V E R   D R O W N I N G

Come in
from the mighty
river, Junior Floyd,
and dry your clothes,

and feed your lungs
the light

from those stricken
seconds just before
the sky rolled,

and bound your
head in thunder.

Now the banks
run six feet low
and it's always
summer.

Some nights
I dream
the river's you.

If you come in
from the raging
Flint, Junior Floyd,

we'll talk of
grown-up things
you never knew.

THE HORN PLAYER'S VERSE

And a great sky descended,
and from it a voice spoke, asking,
'Have you come to count yourself
among the prophets? For only
a prophet may walk here
empty-handed
and his head uncovered.'
I answered I did not and had only
this body, swollen and worn,
to give for the taking of a life
just lived, and again the voice asked,
'Are you then numbered
among the people of the desert
who subsist only that
their song may be each night
lifted to heaven?'
And again I answered, truthfully,
'I know only this body, broken and torn,
given to you for a life just lived,'
speaking then in a fear cold
as the winter cup though the stones
of this very road burned my feet.

THE WINTER PLAINS

PRAYER BEYOND RECOVERY

(Maryland, 1985)

Jimmy Cheese, Jimmy Cheese,
torn jeans and summer flannel sleeves,
city haunted two years for one more fix
to bring you steady and standing alone
off I-95 in rush-hour June,
swearing Bronx by the legs of Mickey Mantle
and all that ever was holy
how the skag and spike and whole fucking works
would be your last, wrapped in a white sock
flung far out over the Patuxent,
free of all temptation.
I say you, Jimmy Cheese,
jailhouse Jesus tats and heart big as a child's—
come down from that bread truck
in North Jersey and bring me back my youth.

CAMILLE (AUGUST 1969)

Then out of a third-floor window
I floated, toward neither land
nor heaven, but just floated

on a mattress slid from their laughter
in the next room, and their glasses
clinking like stars.

You are a good boy, she said,
and don't be afraid,
god looks after good boys,

so I floated out the tangled sky
through high black branches
where drifting bodies curled.

When I closed my eyes
drowned faces stared up at me,
and god is everywhere in all things,

in wind and rain, and the smoke
of electric lines gone down;
in the richelieu, too,

only the richelieu was no more,
so I breathed my own name then
and kept it hid, when he became

all water, calling for the lost.

JUDITH

Tell me, sister, who took
Your name and went with it
To the place of myth and disbelief,
That you might raise

Neither love nor terror
In the hearts of men
Who knew songs of praise
Only for their warrior kings

And no more of sacrifice
Than the blood of cattle?

This is how the sky stood
The night you gave yourself
Beneath a blanched horizon
Bled out for mercy and retribution.

And where are their names written,
In what ground their bones,
Unrepentant and lost,
Those who renounce all

Deliverance by a woman's hand
God-filled in murderous grace?

BENEDICTION

(overheard at Penn Station, Baltimore)

Wipe your face and quit crying,
you still got mustard on your chin.
We all on the same train, baby—
we just gettin off at different places.

SONG FOR THE PHILISTINES

Johnny B wasn't crazy like the farmers said,
just a free spirit who felt the squeeze
in that one-light Nixon town,
how the streets dried up at six o'clock
and the walls closed in and Johnny had to hit
the sidewalks then just to breathe,
walking through town with that long hair
and beard and Jesus sandals because Johnny
refused to drive, walked everywhere he went,
and when the rock festival set up outside of town
in 1970, he walked there too and stayed gone
for three days, and whatever else he didn't find,
he saw Hendrix perform one holy-smoke rendition
of 'The Star-Spangled Banner', it being July 4th and all,
and hippies dropping left and right from
dehydration and bad acid but incredibly
no one died, for which Johnny B was both grateful
and inspired, so on the night of July 8th
(a Wednesday, by the way), he lifted
the lone fifty-gallon trash barrel off Main Street
and took it home and the next day it was back
in place, painted day-glo orange with *rubbish*
stenciled in neat black script, and the pharmacist
wanted Johnny B charged with vandalism, because
in a small town there really are no mysteries,
but the deputy said painting a rusty can
didn't hardly qualify even as a misdemeanor
so that, thanks be to God, Johnny B's rubbish barrel
sat for two years beside a chain-link fence on Main,
right across from the Woodmen of the World.

THE LEAVING HOUSE

These things I cannot tell them
in their kindness, our neighbors
who stop by the front gate
to see what I am planting,
and ask of you (for whom every bud
is an act of annunciation,
each tilt of the spade
a bright parable for the telling).
Theirs are mournful eyes
borrowed from a crucifix; they speak
of suffering and wisdom—and bulbs
do best this time of year, they say.
But I sow my faith in seeds for you
so that a year from now
(two, at the most, he said),
when the pictures on the mantel
have become all strangers to you
and every room a season newly lost,
we will sit together here, and you
will have dusk and flowers in the hands
of a woman unknown to you anymore
and she will tell stories of the moon.

I - 8 1

cattle graze the blue air,
   first coolness of stars—
light in the August grass

J AZZ S ONNET N O . 4

(Bougie Clark, 1956)

If I could bop like Bird or groove like Trane,
couldn't nobody tell me how to step and turn,
Stetson cool, I'd shoot through all that pain,
free tortured souls, and set the rest to burn

An angel of the rooftops brought down by law,
I'd cut and wail, peel back the dying-streets,
a sound that pierced the sky till stars bled raw,
the high throne of New Creation my chosen seat

Landlords, politicians, and the repo men,
Deuce the Roll, silk threads and silver-headed cane,
and uptown narcs, they'd all be lined up end to end
on the lowest rods of a screaming west hell train

If I had Yardbird's hop and Coltrane's smooth,
wouldn't be no doubt, I'd blow the righteous truth

30 LINES FOR JUDAS

Do not imagine that agony
Wears a single aspect—say,
The arched back
Of a hanging man
Or the toothless mouth
Wracked first by denial,
Then by the act itself.
There is yet misery
So profound as to sow
Its own darkness,
Guilt so unspeakable
As to lie beyond admonition,
Abiding in the soul desperate
As roots to a stony,
Waterless ground,
And which will be given
Into your hands alone.
And in this will you forfeit
A quiet heart for a name
Not of your own
Or your father's
Nor any man's choosing,
Waking as if from a dream
To find that you have become
The sound of all words
Imperfectly formed
In every language, reviled even,
And spoken as a curse by those
Upon whose every expression
Is written the mark of deceit.

B U D D Y ' S W O R L D

In the tiny room
where you long ago
became the person
you are
and ever will be,
you took little boy walls
for a full expanse of sky
and corners as a place
where questions
go to die.
Electric blankets
for the sublime,
toy jacks scattered
like stars
across the floor—
but at 28,
do you ever wonder
why you never once
tried the door?

HOMECOMING (SEPTEMBER 1945)

Fresh off the carrier
that brought him stateside
in 1945, Uncle Doyle spent
his only night in Baltimore
down on the Block,
knocking back bourbon and cokes
with a buck private named Roy
from Kingsport, Tennessee.

On the corner of Lombard
and Charles, a peroxide blonde
with a B-movie giggle
and a sailor's cap
promised to take him
Around the world
for ten dollars cash.

Doyle thought about it,
then allowed how he'd seen
too damn much
of the world already,
counted out a dollar fifty
in change and told her
just drop him off in Macon.

THE RETIRED PRIEST
ON GREENMOUNT

(Who Found in Whitman the Word of God)

Nothing I say can diminish you
Whose name is in the language
Of all prayer, a voice
Newly raised in every song
      Do you know the only great
Sin is deliberate cruelty?
       Do you know God is inside
Waiting for you to pray as you will?
Do not defile the sacred
By the easy words of hypocrites
You are the Holy Word
Walking the earth
To be read by all people

YOU IN ANOTHER SEASON . . .

You in another season
were the loveliest of Junes,
a perfect line that bore
the sun straight down
to chlorine light,
then surfaced
on the blinded afternoon.
Time moves slowly
in my blood, dreams
a woman's body wanting
out of the August air—
I hear you laughing still
as your head tilts back,
hands wringing the last
of summer from your hair.

BLUE-IRIS, EARLY SPRING

(Caroline Moore, 1938)

The clerk, a thin balding man
with his apron double strung,
snapped a peppermint stick in half
for tip-toe Frankie and Marielle
while they watched dust motes
tumble across the tin ceiling.
A round, boyish face, he wanted
to know where we were from,
so Marielle said Tennessee
and Frankie lisped the same,
only it sounded like Timothy,
so when he asked if that would be
First or Second, we all laughed
and he handed them each
a piece of licorice.

That was three hours ago,
both girls asleep now in the backseat
beneath an old army blanket.

Frank's eyes remind me
of how it was to stand
at the kitchen window listening
for the far-off call of a freight in winter—
all that dark land and distance,
so I can't tell him I might be.
He says everything that finds its way
down here has its own place to rest—

the osprey and ibis, blue heron. . .
stars even, nested high
in the branches of live oaks.
Frank says soon as he finds work
we'll have a new bed too, cast iron
maybe, and painted white this time.

To Narcissa

I will not ask you
again
about things
you cannot possibly

fathom or scarcely
comprehend

though I suppose
you might begin—
it would be a start
anyway—

by looking into
the water's clear
surface and dropping
a stone straight down.

See if you can find
any depth that way.

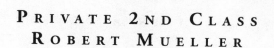

PRIVATE 2ND CLASS
ROBERT MUELLER

(outside Muncie, 1962)

Black dirt and creosote he wore when he was a boy
so we looked there first, the cow pen where he climbed
the rails and trapped wood beetles in a Rumford can—

tried the flatbed wagon and the grain bin too before
Russell found him out there kneeling on the seat just so
he could reach the wheel: 'Why didn't you answer
when you heard us calling you, boy?'

'Busy working,' buzzing his lips like a motor
so Russell laughed the way he did those days, 'Look a there,
Daddy, he's all Mueller, born to the work.'

Korea took him when he was nineteen, place called Taejon.

Now the wheat tops and crows pick the chaff, and each year
the sky grows wider as if it might swallow the whole place
but for the fence line down around the cattle run.
Nothing out there but honeysuckle and briars, a little thistle
and come summer, maybe a wasp nest built on the alternator.

But I can still smell the oil on it, gasoline too, hard smells
to get rid of no matter how long it sits, tires dry rotting,
all the rest gone to rust and weeds and every broken part on it
like a piece of the land that's always belonged.

ELEGY IN A SENSE

When he was 83 years old
and figuring he was about to die,
Elvin Judd lost his left hearing aid.
His wife said it was most likely
deliberate so he'd only hear
about half what was said,
and he said half was more
than enough by a long shot.
Only two things he missed,
he told his nephew Carl
one Saturday while he
was cleaning a Zebco—
his wife's singing voice
and the soft rush of the Kasilof
when the steelhead are running
late August, early fall.
Only thing constant in old age,
he confided, was adjustment
so he kept two
40-year-old Polaroids of Alaska
on the refrigerator door and sat
in the third pew on Sunday
and smiled at the rector, giving thanks
for having already heard
everything needed hearing.

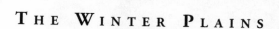

THE WINTER PLAINS

As in a fever then,
In the last hours I heard
The stirring of horses
And in the distance a song
I did not recognize so that

Looking down, I saw a body,
Broken and corrupt, and knew
At once it was my own.
And a voice spoke, saying,

'Do not mourn the absence
Of generations, nor are you
To grieve what is before you,
For it is as the husk cast aside
So that sustenance for the body
May be freely taken.

Go then to serve
All in your presence,
Humblest to the wisest,
To the mightiest in spirit—
You cannot know
His hunger or his need.

Discernment belongs always
To one greater than you.'

INDEX OF FIRST LINES

ABOUT THE AUTHOR

Clif Collins grew up in Byron, Georgia, and attended Clemson University, where he taught full-time from 1988 to 1990. After part-time teaching stints at the Maryland House of Corrections and the Maryland Correctional Institute, he was hired as a member of the English faculty at Montgomery College (Rockville, MD) in 1993. According to Collins, his writing was heavily influenced by the stories he heard as a child from his paternal grandmother and uncles, as well as works he later read by James Baldwin, Lawrence Ferlinghetti, Jack Kerouac, E. L. Doctorow, and Gabriel Garcia Marquez. Equally important to his own work, however, is the tradition of the American singer-songwriter, including Woody Guthrie, Blind Willie McTell, Bob Dylan, John Hiatt, Lucinda Williiams, the Handsome Family, and others. Clif Collins currently resides in Maryland with his wife and son. *Lives of the Apostles* is his first published book.

CPSIA information can be obtained
at www.ICGtesting.com
Printed in the USA
LVHW04s0008021018
592105LV00002B/468/P